A Gift for My Mother

LIDIA MARIA RIBA

Bristol Park Books

First Bristol Park Edition published in 2017.

Bristol Park Books
252 West 38th Street
New York, NY 10018

Bristol Park Books is a registered trademark
of Bristol Park Books, Inc.

Library of Congress Control Number: 2016959778

ISBN: 2016959778

E-Book ISBN: 978-0-88486-640-4

Text and cover design by Keira McGuinness
Cover art copyright ©2017 Guz Anna, Tisha Ardis, Woodhouse/Shutterstock

Printed in Malaysia

To

_____

From

_____

Every son and daughter has probably thought at one time or another:

"Should we tell her how much we love her?
Oh, she already knows…"

"Thank her… 'For what?'
she would say…"

"Let her know?
Oh, she can just imagine…"

And then one day we realize that even if she does know, she has always silently hoped to hear it from us, because she has given us so much, all she could, everything she knew... because she has led us to every path and opened every door.

Because we entered this world, comforted in her embrace.

So, hand in hand, just as when we were little... today is the day to tell her.

for your omnipresence...you managed to come to my piano recital, go to the basketball game and the parent's meeting...all in the same morning.

Thank you...because I can reconstruct my first

years, step by step, by the photographs that

you organized and displayed with such care.

How much love is contained in the pleasure

with which you showed that teary, chocolate-

smeared face?

Thank you because you have always

known how to ask me, "What's wrong?", until

MY WORRIES DISAPPEAR JUST BY SHARING THEM WITH YOU

Thank you for apologizing for the times you were unfair or just plain wrong. You taught me that it takes as much courage to accept mistakes as it does to correct them.

Thank you for clapping and diverting attention from the fact that ...during my recital ...I'd completely forgotten the way my poem ended.

Thank you because you have made me feel that no goal I set for myself is impossible, and because you truly believe it. Your confidence in me has been the best encouragement in my personal growth.

It
Takes
All
Kinds

There are lenient mothers and strict mothers, some are affectionate, others more distant. There are mothers who plan ahead and mothers who improvise, mothers who dedicate every minute to their families and mothers who also have brilliant personal careers. At some point we have reproached our own:

Why doesn't she ever...

Why does she always...

But my friends' mothers...

Yet when we see her with the loving eyes of an adult, we see so much personal courage, her values that we have discovered over the years...and we love her, because that mother, and no other —unique and almost perfect —is our mother.

A MOTHER WHO DOES NOT WORK OUTSIDE THE HOUSE IS A BLESSING

She is always at home when we return. Her voice and the smell of recently baked cookies warm our souls.

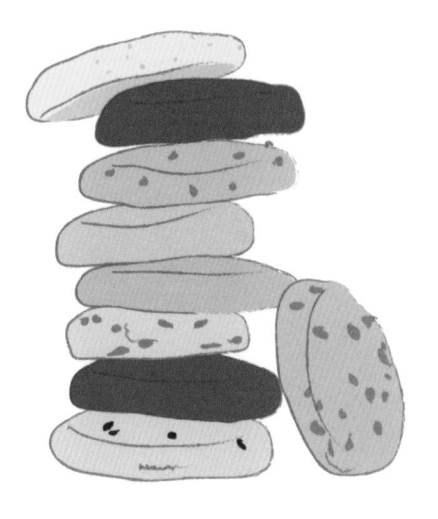

A mother who
works outside
the house is
a blessing

It only takes a little fever for her to postpone everything else, running late and show up a little disheveled. But she will be there.

We know that, no matter what, nothing is more important to her than us.

A
MOTHER
HAS COUNTLESS
PROFESSIONS

She
is
the
nurse

She never flinches at the sight of blood from any wound, the doctor who can tell whether a pain means we are really sick or if there is a hard test at school tomorrow.

SHE
IS THE
BEST
LAWYER

She defends us against teachers and trainers who might be blind to our excellence; the psychologist who quells our fears; the veterinarian who cures our pets (and takes care of them); and the philosopher who helps us understand some of life's eternal mysteries.

Here's to the mothers who have many children, for whom the arrival of each one is a celebration of life. They organize the most complex schedules, take on mountains of laundry, and have traded the pleasures of silence for the loud joy of a home full of kids. They carry out daily miracles of multiplying themselves.

Here's to the mothers of only one child.

Mothers who may have endured years of
waiting, never losing hope, their hearts
overflowing with love for this only child.

Here's to divorced mothers who, from Monday to Friday, watch over homework, wait at the dentist's office, and come and go from karate, piano lessons, and team sports. And when the weekend comes they say goodbye with a smile because Daddy's come to pick up the children.

Here's to the mothers who postponed their dreams and forgot old wounds to stay with the father of their children. Whatever the reasons, and they are numerous, they stay, solid and safe like the lights of a port in a storm.

You
Taught
Me

That there is a loving

and forgiving God.

That love can be infinite

even if it fits inside

one single heart.

That one can have everything in the simple

warmth of a kitchen.

That all roads are possible because you gave

me everything I could possibly need to walk

down them.

That giving, and then giving more without expecting anything in return has made you rich.

That patience is a renewable resource in a mother.

That packing light makes me freer.

That no matter how far my dreams may take me, I can always come home to you.

That discovering my roots do not tether me to the ground, they help me to take off.

That when the flight is rough and I feel like giving up, your love will be the needed gust of wind I need to help me fly higher.

SCENES FROM THE LIFE OF A MOTHER

Frightening nightmares torment her as she lies awake in the middle of the night, waiting for her child to come home. Nightmares vanish with just the sound of a jingle of keys outside the door. Then she smiles and asks, "Did you have a good time?"

"Clean slate, new start," you would say after

my apology followed some self-made disaster.

It was your way of saying the worst was over.

Hearing those magic words I knew I could

move on to something new.

Who else but a mother could unleash so much creativity at eleven o'clock at night, hearing that her child needs a costume as a blooming tree, first thing in the morning for the school play? And who else but Mom, after that sleepless night, would then be seated, front row, center, admiring the best tree in the cast?

Mothers, who are so organized, can make the most detailed shopping list before going to the grocery store...only to come home loaded with things not on her list but that she delighted in as her "great finds".

Only a mother is capable of telling you, as you're heading out to a party: "Maybe we should start a diet together!" And she will also be the first to notice and celebrate your first pound lost.

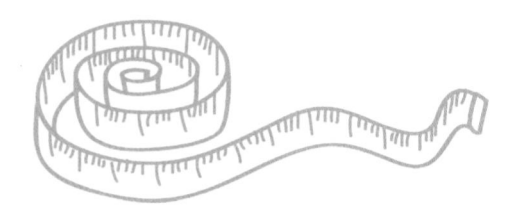

A mother is the one who, at midnight, in a dark house, surrounded by eerie noises, is capable of smiling and, squeezing my hand, say, "Oh, it's nothing. Let's just sing until the power comes back on." Later, much later, we will learn just how scared she was, too.

A woman realizes that she will always be a mother when, on her way out the door after an argument, having decided to leave and not come back for a few hours, finds herself making a long list of recommendations:

the baby needs her cough medicine

at twelve...

...it has to be administered slowly;

don't forget her lotion...

...she should be changed in an hour.

— and it's unlikely that she will actually leave.

I
Remember

That you learned how to drive just so you

could pick me up from school.

That the dentist always rewarded me with a

new storybook...that you had sneaked in to his

assistant.

That your budget could stretch a little bit more

when I wanted those shiny shoes more than

anything in the world.

That you cleaned up my wreck of a teenage bedroom *"Just this once!"* you said, over and over again.

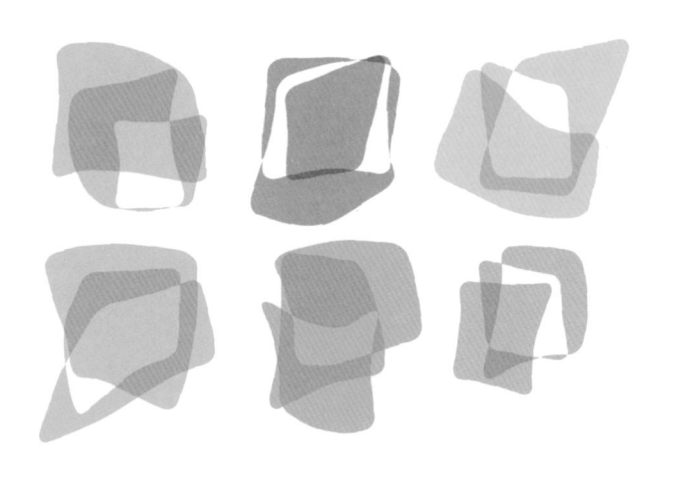

I WILL NEVER FORGET

That there was not a single minute when

I couldn't count on your support (not your

approval, for we disagreed often). But I always

knew I wasn't alone, that you were there to

soften my fall or celebrate my success.

That you never spoke to me about honesty,

the importance of hard work or generosity. But

those values are still ingrained in me because

I've watched you live according to them

throughout my life.

That you were never too busy to listen to me,

too tired to help me, too worried about your

own problems to understand mine, or too

serious to laugh with me.

Stay

With

Me

On my first day of school...

When I fall in love for the first time...

When I love and am not loved back...

When the sun, the music, and the splendor make me forget to call you...

When I am overcome by pain and utter your name wordlessly...

When each of my children is born...

When they grow up and leave...

When I'm surrounded by people, but feel alone...

When I miss my loved ones...

And when you finally do have to go.

Mother, let's play a trick on fate: stay with me forever, hidden in my soul.

I

FORGIVE

YOU

For the times you stole my friends' attention by telling cool stories about when you were young.

For telling me a lot of things for my own good, that I would have preferred not to hear.

For standing up and yelling "Bravo, Bravo!" in the silence of the school hall when I came in sixth place in the drawing contest. I wanted to disappear on the spot. Now the memory of that moment has become very precious to me.

For not knowing how to bake muffins, but never forgetting my favorites when you went to the grocery store. Desserts, you can buy; love, you cannot.

Just
Between
Us

Now I know your secrets.

I know that in your heart you hid

secret dreams...that you had hopes...and

desires...but you kept them to yourself.

You never let the wings of those thoughts

brush against my own flight. You let me lift off

without tying me down, and I never suspected

until much later that you might have also

yearned for the horizon.

The love of a child goes from exclusive

adoration in infancy, to harsh criticism during

adolescence; then to a fond distance as our

own adult world absorbs and distracts us. If we

have a child of our own, a magical circle of

love is completed.

Then we can see and understand so much of ourselves in our mothers. Thank you, Mother, for waiting, patiently, for that magical circle to close.

How wonderful it is that the day has finally come when we can also be friends. We share the pleasure of ordinary adventures:

Lunches alone in a restaurant, (so much to talk and laugh about), shopping sprees and long talks on the phone. Your presence is a most important gift to my life. Your love has taught me to see and enjoy the good things that life has in store for me.

What can I give you in exchange?

Only my words, limited and inadequate.

Mom, may your heart listen to my heart, telling you, simply, thank you

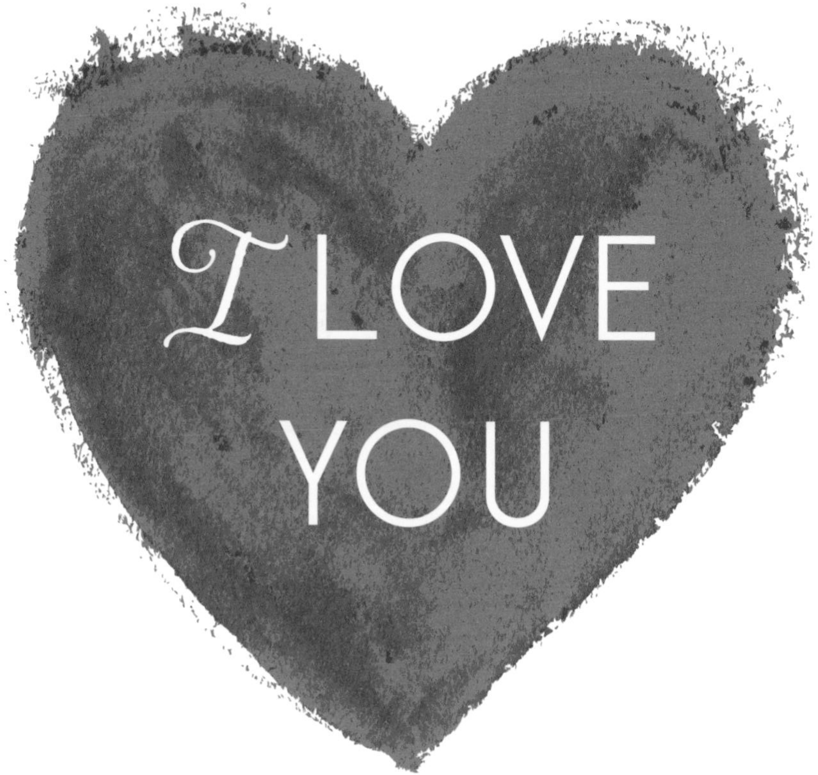
I LOVE
YOU

Illustration Credits